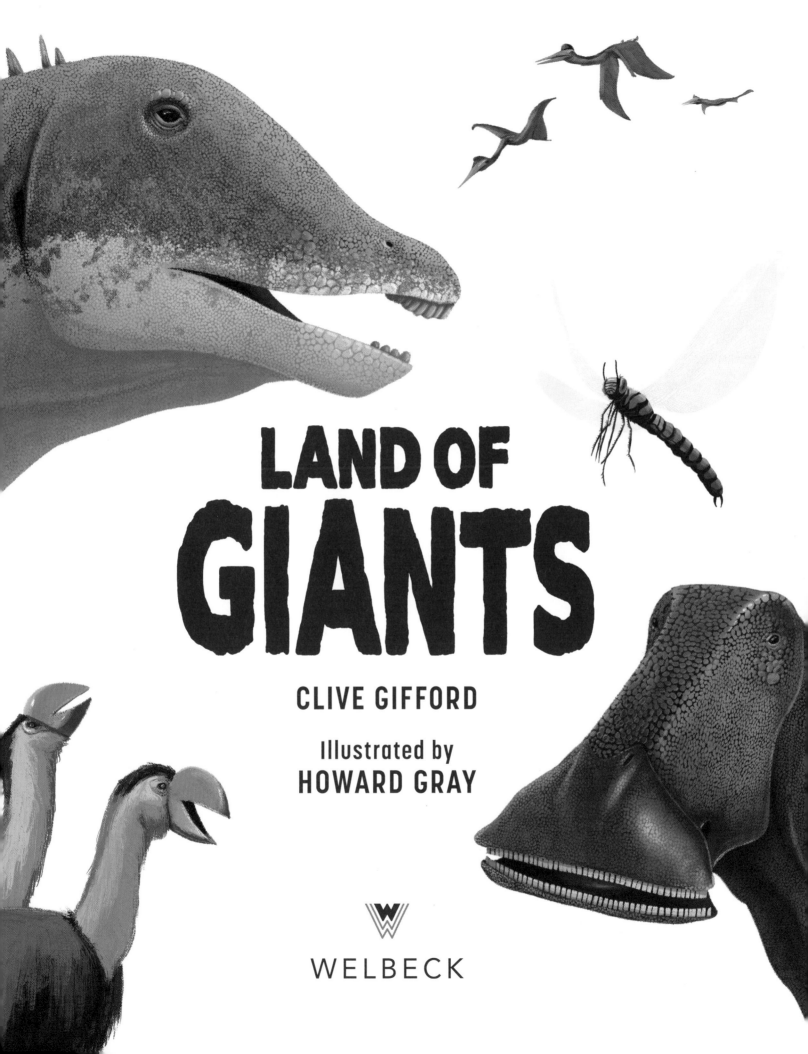

LAND OF GIANTS

CLIVE GIFFORD

Illustrated by
HOWARD GRAY

WELBECK

Published in 2022 by Welbeck Children's Books
An imprint of Welbeck Children's Limited,
part of Welbeck Publishing Group.
Based in London and Sydney.

www.welbeckpublishing.com

Consultant Paleontologist: Chris Barker

ISBN 978 1 78312 850 1

Printed in Heshan, China
10 9 8 7 6 5 4 3 2

FSC
www.fsc.org
MIX
Paper | Supporting
responsible forestry
FSC® C020056

CONTENTS

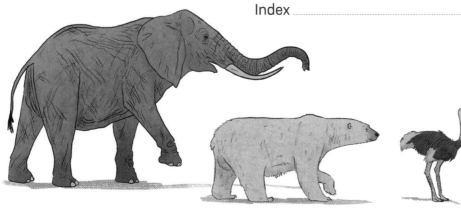

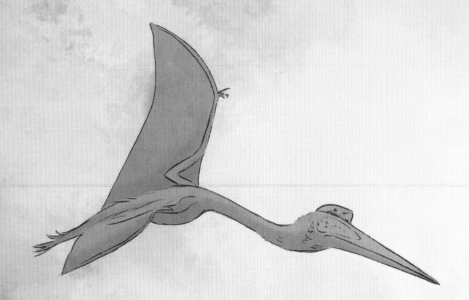

STEP INTO THE LAND OF GIANTS

Welcome to the world of big, BIG beasts.

Life on Earth began in the water and stayed incredibly tiny for billions of years. Gradually, larger creatures developed, first in the seas then on land. Some of these living things evolved over millions and millions of years into giants. Dinosaurs, for example, arrived around 240 million years ago. These reptiles, some of which grew to extraordinary sizes, dominated life on land for millions of years. But dinosaurs weren't the only huge creatures on the planet at that time. There were also enormous fish and reptiles in the seas and monstrous flying reptiles in the skies as well.

Scientists who study prehistoric life rely on detective work to piece together the bones and evidence they find. How creatures looked, their size, weight, and living habits are estimated from all the evidence.

Since the time of the dinosaurs, many other giant creatures have come and gone, including birds twice your height, huge pigs, rabbits and beavers, and a rhinoceros almost the size of a school bus. Why did so many creatures get so big? Sometimes, it gave them an advantage such as being able to reach taller plants or eat more food in a single sitting. Being larger could also offer greater protection against predators—creatures which hunt other creatures for food.

This book is packed with some of the biggest animals, birds, fish, and insects to ever live, from creatures around before the time of the dinosaurs to those giants who live with us today. So what are you waiting for? Let's take a journey through time on Planet Earth: the Land of Giants...

GIANTS OF THE FORESTS & PLAINS

Over millions of years, many strange and powerful giants evolved to live on plains and in forests around the world. One such beast was *Josephoartigasia monesi* (Jo-sef-fo-ar-teh-gay-sha mon-ess-ee), which could be found roaming these landscapes between two and four million years ago. It was the biggest ever rodent and dwarfed mice and rats. Its head alone was over 20 inches (50 cm) long and the whole creature may have weighed hundreds of pounds.

Sauropods

Sauropods were the largest of all dinosaurs. All were four-legged plant eaters with incredibly long necks to reach tall tree leaves which they ate in huge quantities. Their legs needed to be incredibly strong and sturdy to support their great weight.

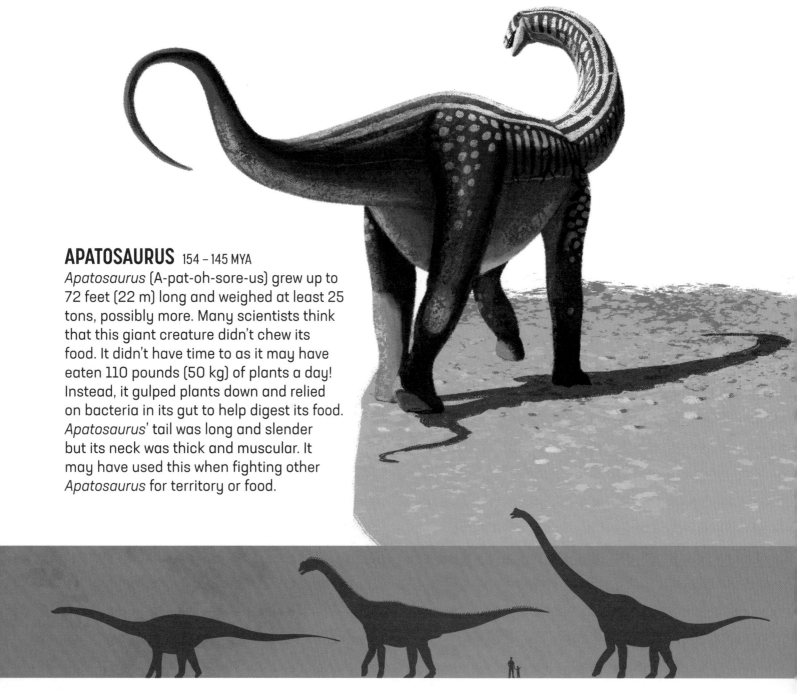

APATOSAURUS 154 – 145 MYA

Apatosaurus (A-pat-oh-sore-us) grew up to 72 feet (22 m) long and weighed at least 25 tons, possibly more. Many scientists think that this giant creature didn't chew its food. It didn't have time to as it may have eaten 110 pounds (50 kg) of plants a day! Instead, it gulped plants down and relied on bacteria in its gut to help digest its food. *Apatosaurus'* tail was long and slender but its neck was thick and muscular. It may have used this when fighting other *Apatosaurus* for territory or food.

CAMARASAURUS 155 – 145 MYA

Herds of *Camarasaurus* (Cam-ah-rah-sore-us) roamed North America. Adults grew between 50 and 75 feet (15 to 23 m) long. Inside its almost square-shaped head were spoon-shaped teeth. These were able to cut and chew through even the toughest leaves, twigs, and branches.

BRACHIOSAURUS 155 – 145 MYA

Brachiosaurus (Brak-he-o-sore-us) was a particularly large sauroprod. Each of its thigh bones were taller than a man and the whole creature could grow up to 66 feet (20 m) long—nearly as long as a blue whale. Its extremely long neck allowed its mouth to reach leaves high above the ground, out of the range of other creatures.

Argentinosaurus 97 – 94 MYA

In 1987, a farmer in Argentina, tilling his land, discovered a giant prehistoric bone. A big dig was organized and more bones were found. They were part of one of the largest creatures ever to roam on land.

A female *Argentinosaurus* (Ar-jen-teen-oh-sore-us) laid at least half a dozen eggs, each around the size and shape of a football. From each egg hatched a baby that weighed about ten pounds (4.5 kg). Eating a lot of plants, it grew at an incredible rate to become a truly monstrous beast as an adult.

We don't have an entire *Argentinosaurus* skeleton, so scientists make estimates from the bones they have. These include a femur (leg bone) which measures over eight feet (2.5 m) long. They estimate that an adult *Argentinosaurus* may have measured 100 to 120 feet (30 to 37 m) long—longer than a Boeing 737 jet airliner. It was heavier than the airliner, too. We think it weighed up to 88 tons—the weight of 17 monster trucks or over 1,000 people!

TITANOSAURS

Argentinosaurus is one of a group of enormous sauropods called titanosaurs. New titanosaur bones are being discovered all the time, so there may be a prehistoric land creature even bigger than *Argentinosaurus* out there.

Big Frills, Big Thrills

Ceratopsians were a family of plant-eating dinosaurs with toothless beaks and, in later species, huge frills and horns. They first appeared around 140 million years ago and many lived in herds on the plains. Banding together helped protect individuals from hungry predators.

TRICERATOPS 70 – 66 MYA

Triceratops (Try-seh-ra-tops) is the most famous ceratopsian. It was built like a giant, heavy rhinoceros, growing up to 30 feet (9 m) long and weighing nearly eight tons. Its head was enormous and made up as much as a third of the length of its body. What made it seem even larger was a large bony frill that surrounded the back and sides of its head. Used to attract mates, the frill certainly helped make the head heavy. As a result, *Triceratops* mostly ate plants which grew low or on the ground.

The dinosaur had a short horn on its nose covered in the same material, keratin, that forms your fingernails. Its two bigger horns stuck out from above its eyes and could be around three feet (1 m) long. *Triceratops* occasionally used these to defend itself against hostile dinosaurs but mostly to fight other *Triceratops*. The horns were sharp and could cause serious injury.

STYRACOSAURUS 76 – 70 MYA

This 18-foot-long (5.5 m) ceratopsian's nose contained one 24-inch-long (60 cm) thick horn sticking out of its nose and two more sticking out of its cheeks. That wasn't all. Around its bony frill were a further six sharp spikes giving *Styracosaurus* (Sti-ra-ko-sore-us) a really scary appearance.

Giants with Claws and Spikes

These bulky dinosaurs had fearsome-looking weapons, but they were rarely used in anger. Experts believe they were largely peaceful plant eaters.

THERIZINOSAURUS 70.6 – 66 MYA
The strange looking *Therizinosaurus* (Ther-ih-zeen-oh-sore-us) had a beak, a large pot belly and a body and tail partly covered in feathers. The largest measured around 26 feet (8 m) long—about the length of two cars—and weighed more than a rhinoceros. At the end of its eight-foot-long (2.4 m) arms was its most unusual body part: three phenomenally long claws. Most creatures' claws measure an inch or two—*Therizinosaurus*' claws grew more than 20 inches (50 cm) long. These may have been used to hook and pull vegetation toward its mouth.

STEGOSAURUS 155 – 150 MYA

Large and lumbering, *Stegosaurus* (Steg-oh-sare-us) couldn't have moved much faster than you out on a brisk walk. This four-legged plant muncher measured up to 30 feet (9 m) long—longer than two cars bumper to bumper. Young ones could have been a target for giant hunting dinosaurs, but it did have a defense. At the end of its muscular tail was a thagomizer made up of four large, pointed spikes. These would have inflicted a nasty wound if they struck another creature.

A row of 19 large bony plates called scutes ran all the way along *Stegosaurus*' back. The plates were covered in keratin and had pipe-like blood vessels inside. Being so high up on the back, these probably weren't used for defense, and instead may have helped *Stegosaurus* attract mates.

Quetzalcoatlus 68 – 66 MYA

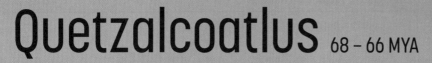

Pterosaurs were flying reptiles that lived on Earth at the same time as dinosaurs. Some were small. *Nemicolopterus* (nem-ee-col-op-ter-us), for example, had a wingspan of nne to ten inches (22-25 cm)— little more than a house sparrow. At the other end of the scale, was the biggest flying creature the world has ever seen. It was named after an Aztec god which took the form of a serpent with feathers...

Quetzalcoatlus (Kwet-zal-co-at-lass) had a wingspan of 36 feet (11 m). That's about the same as a World War II fighter plane or a light aircraft today. Everything about this extraordinary flying reptile was super-sized. This included its 6.5-foot-long (2 m) neck and its eight-foot-long (2.5 m) head, which was mostly beak. Just imagine having a head almost twice as long as you are tall!

Quetzalcoatlus weighed about 530 pounds (240 kg). We think it would launch itself into the air using both its legs and its clawed wings. What a sight take-off must have been. Once in flight, *Quetzalcoatlus* probably used its huge wings, made of skin stiffened with fibers, to soar over land like big birds do today. It may have covered hundreds of miles in a single flight.

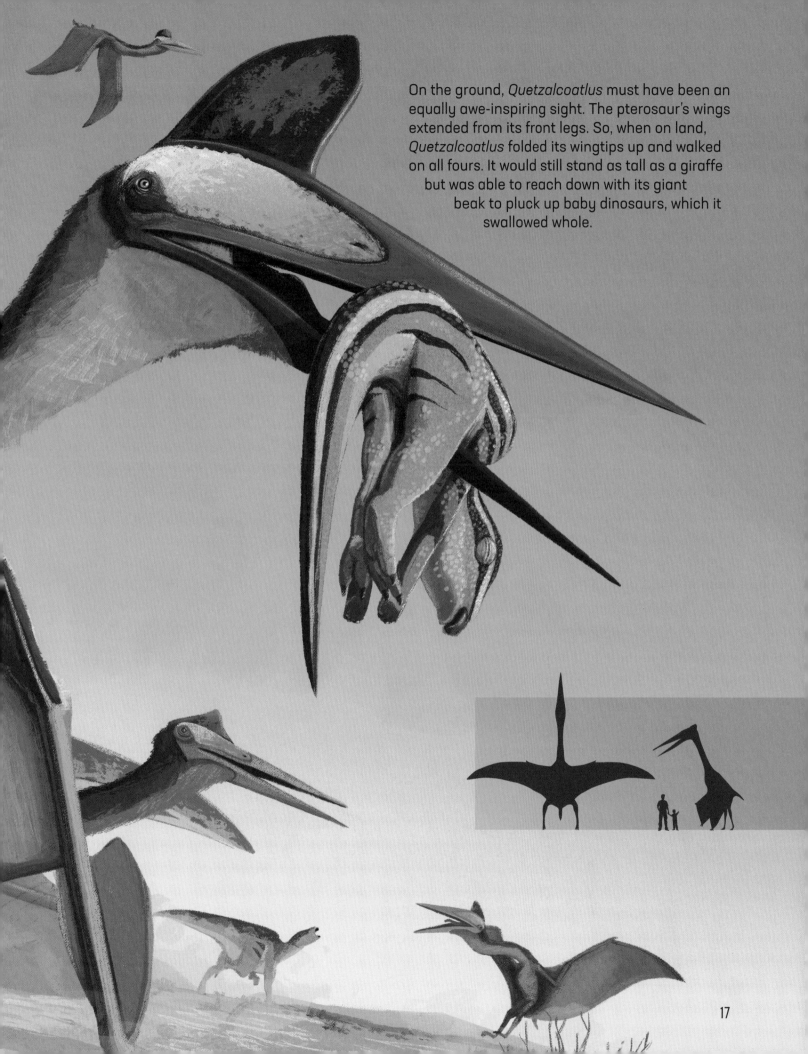

On the ground, *Quetzalcoatlus* must have been an equally awe-inspiring sight. The pterosaur's wings extended from its front legs. So, when on land, *Quetzalcoatlus* folded its wingtips up and walked on all fours. It would still stand as tall as a giraffe but was able to reach down with its giant beak to pluck up baby dinosaurs, which it swallowed whole.

17

Big Eaters

Giant creatures need a lot of food to survive. A titanosaur may have eaten hundreds of pounds of food every day. Scientists study fossils of a creature's head, mouth, and teeth to help figure out what sort of food they most likely ate.

TYRANNOSAURUS REX

68 – 66 MYA

Lots of sharp teeth with jagged edges like a saw are found in *Tyrannosaurus rex*'s mouth. These indicate that it was a meat eater. It used its teeth and powerful jaws to tear big chunks of flesh away. In contrast, many giant prehistoric plant eaters had lots of big, blocky teeth. These helped grind food down as the creature chewed.

Poops can become rock-hard fossils, too! They are called coprolites and are also studied by scientists to learn more about ancient creatures' feeding habits.

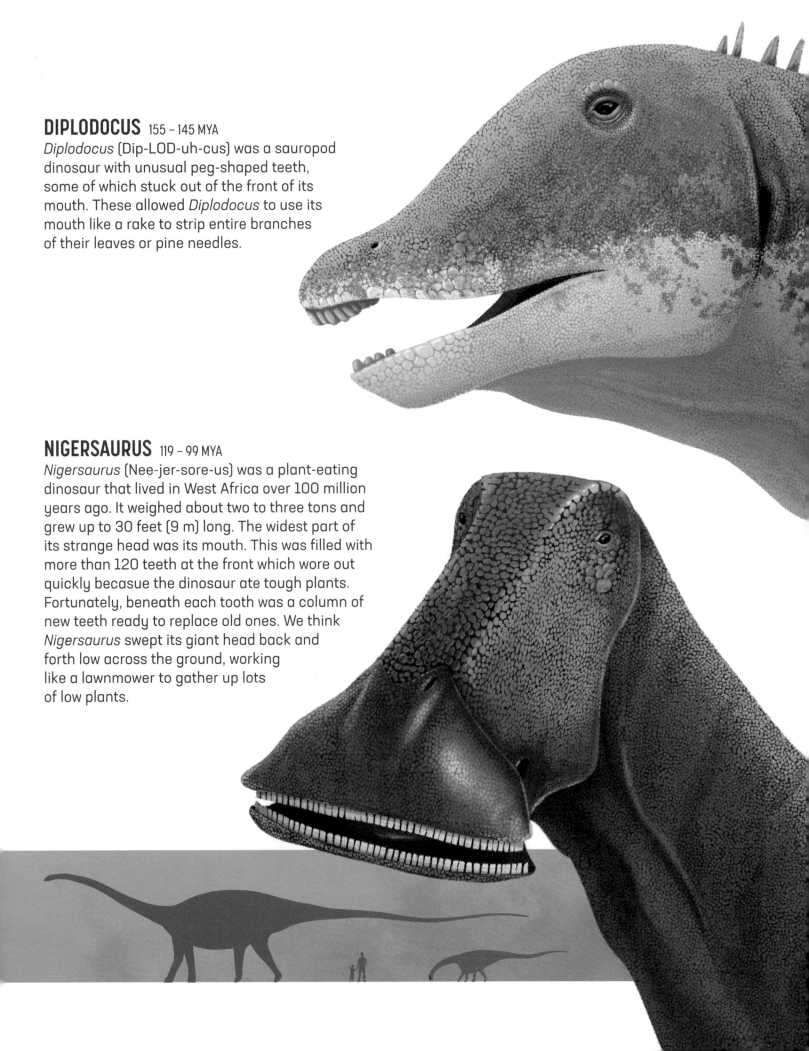

DIPLODOCUS 155 – 145 MYA

Diplodocus (Dip-LOD-uh-cus) was a sauropod dinosaur with unusual peg-shaped teeth, some of which stuck out of the front of its mouth. These allowed *Diplodocus* to use its mouth like a rake to strip entire branches of their leaves or pine needles.

NIGERSAURUS 119 – 99 MYA

Nigersaurus (Nee-jer-sore-us) was a plant-eating dinosaur that lived in West Africa over 100 million years ago. It weighed about two to three tons and grew up to 30 feet (9 m) long. The widest part of its strange head was its mouth. This was filled with more than 120 teeth at the front which wore out quickly becasue the dinosaur ate tough plants. Fortunately, beneath each tooth was a column of new teeth ready to replace old ones. We think *Nigersaurus* swept its giant head back and forth low across the ground, working like a lawnmower to gather up lots of low plants.

Largest Ever Land Mammals

Millions of years after the dinosaurs died out, big beasts roamed the land once more. Relatives of elephants and especially rhinos grew to some awe-inspiring sizes.

PARACERATHERIUM 34 – 23 MYA

Paraceratherium (Para-sera-theer-ee-um) was an extraordinary hornless rhino found grazing in open woodlands and plains of Eurasia. Fossils of this creature have been found in Bulgaria, India, and China.

What made *Paraceratherium* extraordinary was its sheer size; it was almost as big as an entire bus. Scientists estimate that at the top of its shoulders the creature stood 16 feet (4.8 m) above the ground. A human could stand between the creature's two pairs of long legs and still would have to reach up with their hands to touch its belly. The entire creature weighed around 20 tons—more than three adult elephants. That is heavy.

Paraceratherium's great height, plus its long neck, meant its head could reach branches off the ground. This meant it could graze the tops of trees that other animals of the time couldn't reach. Its large front teeth would strip all the leaves and berries from branches. To feed that enormous frame would have taken around-the-clock eating.

ASIAN STRAIGHT-TUSKED ELEPHANT 5.3 MYA – 11,000 years ago

Species of giant prehistoric elephant roamed the plains of Europe and Asia in the past. This particular species, whose scientific name is *Palaeoloxodon namadicus* (Pay-leo-lox-oh-don na-mad-ick-us), was found in India and China. It may have been the largest land mammal of all time. Experts estimate it stood 15 feet (4.5 m) tall at the shoulder at least. The largest adult males may have weighed as much as 24 tons –four times the weight of elephants today.

A bony crest ran round its skull a little like a headband. Large muscles may have attached to this bone to help support the creature's large head. On either side of its trunk grew large tusks which were straight, although some curved just before their tips.

North American Plains Giants

Long after the dinosaurs died out, some large mammals evolved to take their place as the largest creatures in North America.

SHORT-FACED BEAR 1.8 MYA – 11,000 years ago
The short-faced bear was the largest meat-eating mammal to ever roam North America. Up to 12 feet (3.7 m) tall when standing on its rear legs, it would have towered over a person. Even when on all fours, its head would be as far off the ground as an adult man's. Some male short-faced bears weighed as much as 2,200 pounds (1,000 kg)—more than twice the weight of a grizzly bear.

The bear had a wide snout filled with long, pointed canine teeth at the front of its mouth and blocky molar teeth at the back. Scientists think it ate a wide range of food including bison, deer, and fruits. Its large size may have helped it to muscle in on carcasses, driving away smaller hunters and scavengers.

CASTOROIDES 1.8 MYA – 12,000 years ago
Castoroides (Cass-tor-oy-dees) was a giant beaver, with a 6.5-foot-long (2 m) body covered in shaggy hair. It is the biggest rodent ever discovered in North America. It weighed between 175 and 220 pounds (80 and 100 kg)—about five times as heavy as a modern beaver! At the front of its mouth were huge, curved cutting teeth that would chomp through plants with ease. These teeth were a whopping six inches (15 cm) long. Measure your teeth with a ruler to compare.

DAEODON 30 – 20 MYA

Daeodon (Day-oh-don) was a huge creature as big as the short-faced bear. It might be a relavite of hippos and whales. Weighing over 1,750 pounds (800 kg) and standing as tall as one of your teachers, it must have been a fearsome sight. It ate both plants and meat and sometimes used its powerful jaws and big teeth on other *Daeodons*, judging by bite marks found on skeletons. The North American plains and forests must have suited this monstrous creature, because it thrived there for around 10 million years.

Australian Giants

Just like today with its koalas, kangaroos, and duck-billed platypus, Australia was home to some incredible creatures in the distant past.

STIRTON'S THUNDER BIRD 8 – 7 MYA

Dromornithids (Dro-more-nith-ids) were a group of huge, flightless birds only found in prehistoric Australia. Stirton's Thunder Bird was the biggest of the gang, towering 10 feet (3 m) high and weighing around 1,100 pounds (500 kg)—the weight of three ostriches. The bird had large, blunt claws, a sturdy pair of legs, and a giant 20-inch-long (50 cm) head. Despite their enormous size, thunder birds are related to modern waterfowl such as ducks and geese.

DIPROTODON 1.6 MYA – 44,000 years ago

Plant-eating *Diprotodon* (Di-proe-toe-don) was the world's largest wombat. This marsupial (which carried its young in a pouch) weighed more than a large car and stood on four stout legs the size of tree trunks. It was more than ten feet (3 m) long and had a big, thick skull with a large nose.

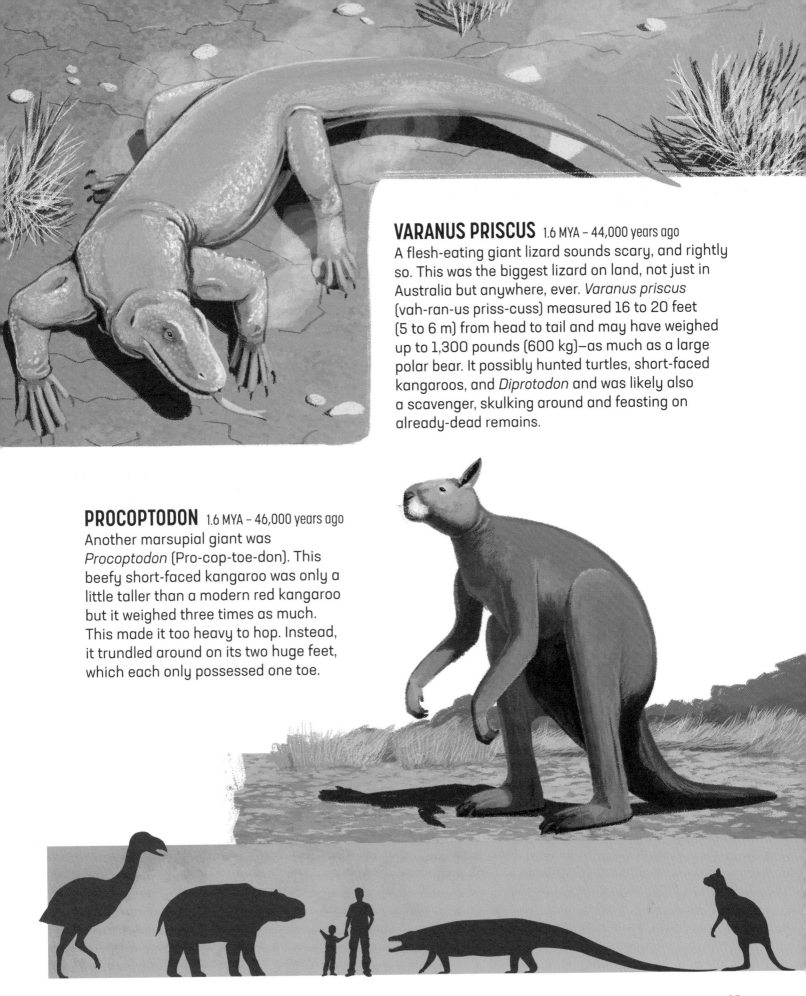

VARANUS PRISCUS 1.6 MYA – 44,000 years ago

A flesh-eating giant lizard sounds scary, and rightly so. This was the biggest lizard on land, not just in Australia but anywhere, ever. *Varanus priscus* (vah-ran-us priss-cuss) measured 16 to 20 feet (5 to 6 m) from head to tail and may have weighed up to 1,300 pounds (600 kg)—as much as a large polar bear. It possibly hunted turtles, short-faced kangaroos, and *Diprotodon* and was likely also a scavenger, skulking around and feasting on already-dead remains.

PROCOPTODON 1.6 MYA – 46,000 years ago

Another marsupial giant was *Procoptodon* (Pro-cop-toe-don). This beefy short-faced kangaroo was only a little taller than a modern red kangaroo but it weighed three times as much. This made it too heavy to hop. Instead, it trundled around on its two huge feet, which each only possessed one toe.

Giants of South America

Long after the dinosaurs died out, the prehistoric plains and forests of South America were home to some extraordinary and enormous creatures.

GLYPTODONTS 35 MYA – 11,700 years ago

Glyptodonts (Glip-toe-donts) were related to modern armadillos, but much bigger! Some were about the size of a Volkswagen Beetle car but weighing twice as much. Plates of armor covered their entire body and their tail. Some even had a patch of bony armor on the top of their heads.

Several glyptodont species used their tails when they fought each other over resources. They would swing them like a hefty club and crunch into their opponent's head and body. Ouch!

Glyptodont feet were funny. The rear toes had hoof-like claws that helped to support their weight, whereas the front pair had five toes each ending in a short claw. Experts don't think glyptodonts were fussy eaters. They would gobble plants, grinding them down with their blocky teeth.

MEGATHERIUM 3.6 MYA – 8,000 years ago

Glyptodonts lived alongside prehistoric sloths that also foraged for plants on the ground. Sloths alive today are under 2.5 feet (80 cm) long and weigh less than 18 pounds (8 kg). Imagine a sloth as tall as an elephant and as heavy as two cars! *Megatherium* (Meg-ah-theer-ee-um) could reach 11 feet (3.5 m) in height when it stood up on its rear legs and weighed about four tons.

When standing on all fours, *Megatherium* may have been as long as 23 feet (7 m), from nose to tail. This beefy creature had to walk on the sides of its feet as its curved claws, which were good for stripping leaves from branches, stopped its feet from standing flat on the ground.

Northern Giants

We think of the northern and polar regions of Earth as being bitterly cold lands of frost and snow. But through Earth's history, the North has at times been warmer and at other times colder than it is today. As the climate changed, different animals made it their home.

HIGH ARCTIC CAMEL 3.5 MYA

Some 3.5 million years ago, the High Arctic Camel lived deep within the Arctic Circle which at the time contained grasslands and wintry forests of larch trees—quite different from the dry, baking heat of the deserts where we find camels today!

This giant camel had a single fatty hump and stood about nine feet (2.8 m) tall at its shoulder, up to a third taller than current camels. It may have weighed as much as 2,000 pounds (900 kg) —the weight of three grizzly bears—at the end of summer after feeding itself up to survive the cold winters when less food was around.

MEGALOCEROS 2.59 MYA – 12,000 years ago

Megaloceros giganteus (Meg-ah-loe-seh-ross gi-gan-tee-us) roamed over parts of northern Europe and Asia. To prehistoric people, the giant deer must have been an impressive sight. It stood taller than them at 6.5 feet (2 m) to its shoulder and was about eight feet (2.5 m) long. That's about the same length as an elk today, but *Megaloceros* was around twice as heavy. What really made it stand out, though, was its phenomenal antlers. These could weigh about 90 pounds (40 kg) and span 12.5 feet (3.8 m) wide—far wider than the creature was long. Experts believe that male deer used these to battle over females during mating season.

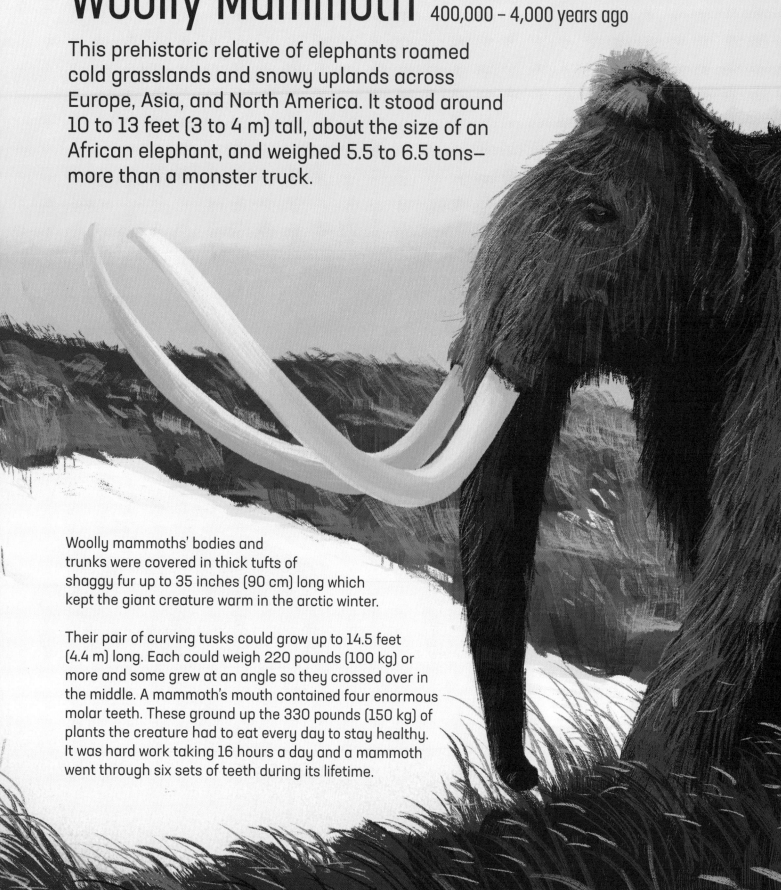

Woolly Mammoth

400,000 – 4,000 years ago

This prehistoric relative of elephants roamed cold grasslands and snowy uplands across Europe, Asia, and North America. It stood around 10 to 13 feet (3 to 4 m) tall, about the size of an African elephant, and weighed 5.5 to 6.5 tons—more than a monster truck.

Woolly mammoths' bodies and trunks were covered in thick tufts of shaggy fur up to 35 inches (90 cm) long which kept the giant creature warm in the arctic winter.

Their pair of curving tusks could grow up to 14.5 feet (4.4 m) long. Each could weigh 220 pounds (100 kg) or more and some grew at an angle so they crossed over in the middle. A mammoth's mouth contained four enormous molar teeth. These ground up the 330 pounds (150 kg) of plants the creature had to eat every day to stay healthy. It was hard work taking 16 hours a day and a mammoth went through six sets of teeth during its lifetime.

Mammoths could get the hump—a large fatty hump on their backs. This acted as a food store for the creatures during lean times in winter when food was scarce. Injured and infant mammoths were sometimes hunted for food by packs of prehistoric wolves and by some early peoples armed with sharpened stick spears.

Woolly mammoths died out around 10-11,000 years ago. Well, almost all of them did. A small population of mammoths continued to live on Wrangle Island—deep in the Arctic Ocean and north of Russia—until around 4,000 years ago. So, woolly mammoths still existed after the ancient Egyptian pyramids had been built.

Island Giants

Prehistoric islands were peculiar places to live on. There were no people and few or no large predators. Stuck in the same place for millions of years, some animals evolved to become larger than their relatives on the mainland. This is known as island gigantism.

Creatures caught on an island could only live off the plants and animals it contained. They couldn't roam elsewhere. For some species, this was a problem and they died out, but for others, they could grow bigger and bigger. This especially occurred if island creatures had plenty of plants and other food to eat and weren't threatened by big predators.

NURALAGUS REX 5.3 – 3.6 MYA
Island gigantism happened on the Mediterranean island of Minorca. It became home to one big bunny around three to five million years ago. *Nuralagus rex* (Noor-ah-lay-gus rex) was about six times the size of a modern rabbit and weighed up to 31 pounds (14 kg).

BLUNT-TOOTHED GIANT HUTIA
Around 500,000 years ago
On the Caribbean island of Anguilla, a relative of mice and rats called the blunt-toothed giant hutia grew to weigh up to 440 pounds (200 kg) and was almost the size of a bear.

DEINOGALERIX 11.6 – 5.3 MYA
Gargano is now part of Italy, but in the past it was an island. It contained a number of giant creatures including *Deinogalerix* (Die-no-ga-le-rix). This giant, hairy hedgehog was 24 inches (60 cm) long. Deinogalerix lived off insects and other small creatures. It didn't need spiky spines for protection as there were few big predators, so it didn't grow them!

ISLAND DWARFISM
For some big creatures stuck on an island, the only solution was to evolve into smaller and smaller versions which needed less food. In prehistoric Cyprus, tiny dwarf elephants existed which weighed 440 pounds (200 kg)—more than twenty times lighter than an African elephant.

541 **485** **44**

PROTEROZOIC

PALEOPROTEROZOIC MESOPROTEROZOIC NEOPROTEROZOIC

Cambrian Ordovician

550 MYA:
first animals with shells

500 MYA:
first land plants evolve

2,000 MYA:
multicellular life evolves

530 MYA:
first fishes evolve

535 MYA:
many different living things evolve in a short
time, known as the "Cambrian explosion"

ARGENTINOSAURUS **THERIZINOSAURUS** **VARANUS PRISCUS**

Colossal Body Bits

Some prehistoric creatures were gigantic overall.
Others had particularly big body parts or laid HUGE eggs.

OPHTHALMOSAURUS 165 – 150 MYA

Ophthalmosaurus (Of-thal-moe-sore-us) was a scary sea hunter. It was shaped like a giant dolphin and prowled the ocean, possibly as far down as 2,000 feet (600 m). At those depths, there's little sunlight so *Ophthalmosaurus* needed all the help its giant eyes could give it. These measured nine inches (23 cm) wide —bigger than a soccer ball. The pair of eyeballs filled the creature's skull. There was only just enough room to cram in its brain as well!

AEPYORNIS 12,000 – 1,000 years ago

Aepyornis (Ay-pe-or-nis) was also known as the elephant bird, and with good reason. It stood ten feet (3 m) tall, weighed about 1,000 pounds (450 kg) (more than four giant pandas), and laid big, BIG eggs. You'd need a piece of string more than three feet long (1 m) to reach all the way around a single *Aepyornis* egg, which had 150 times the volume of a chicken's egg. When humans reached Madagascar a few thousand years ago, they found that a single *Aepyornis* egg could feed a large family easily.

TIMELINE OF LIFE ON EARTH

Earth's long history is divided up into geological time periods called eons, eras, and periods. Life on Earth may have began over three billion years ago but it was only in the past 300 million years—in the Palaeozoic, Mesozoic, and Cenozoic eras—that creatures evolved to truly enormous sizes.

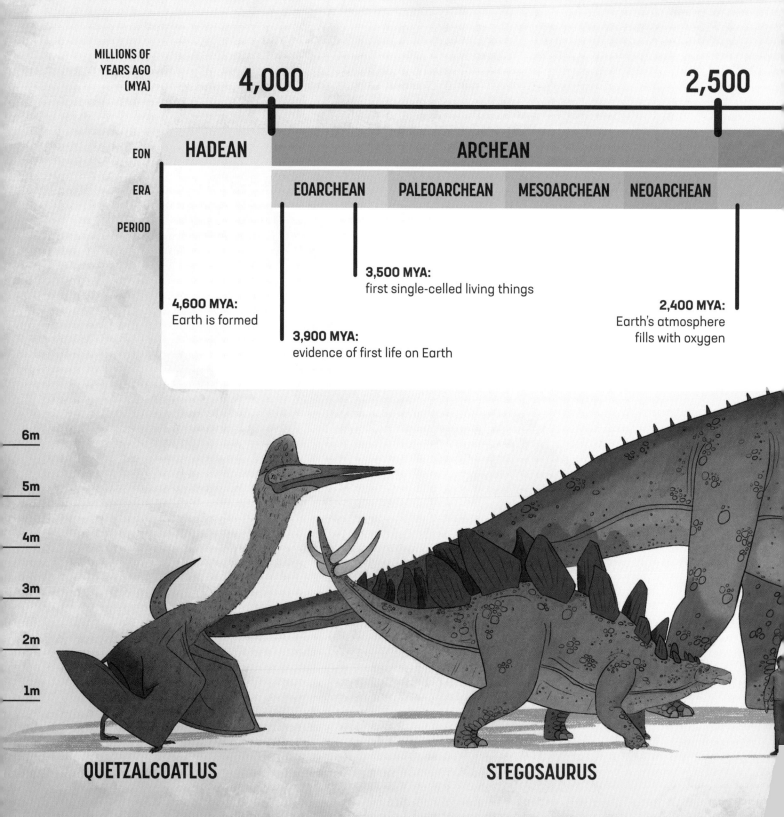

MILLIONS OF YEARS AGO (MYA)

4,000

2,500

EON	HADEAN	ARCHEAN			
ERA		EOARCHEAN	PALEOARCHEAN	MESOARCHEAN	NEOARCHEAN
PERIOD					

3,500 MYA:
first single-celled living things

4,600 MYA:
Earth is formed

3,900 MYA:
evidence of first life on Earth

2,400 MYA:
Earth's atmosphere fills with oxygen

6m
5m
4m
3m
2m
1m

QUETZALCOATLUS

STEGOSAURUS

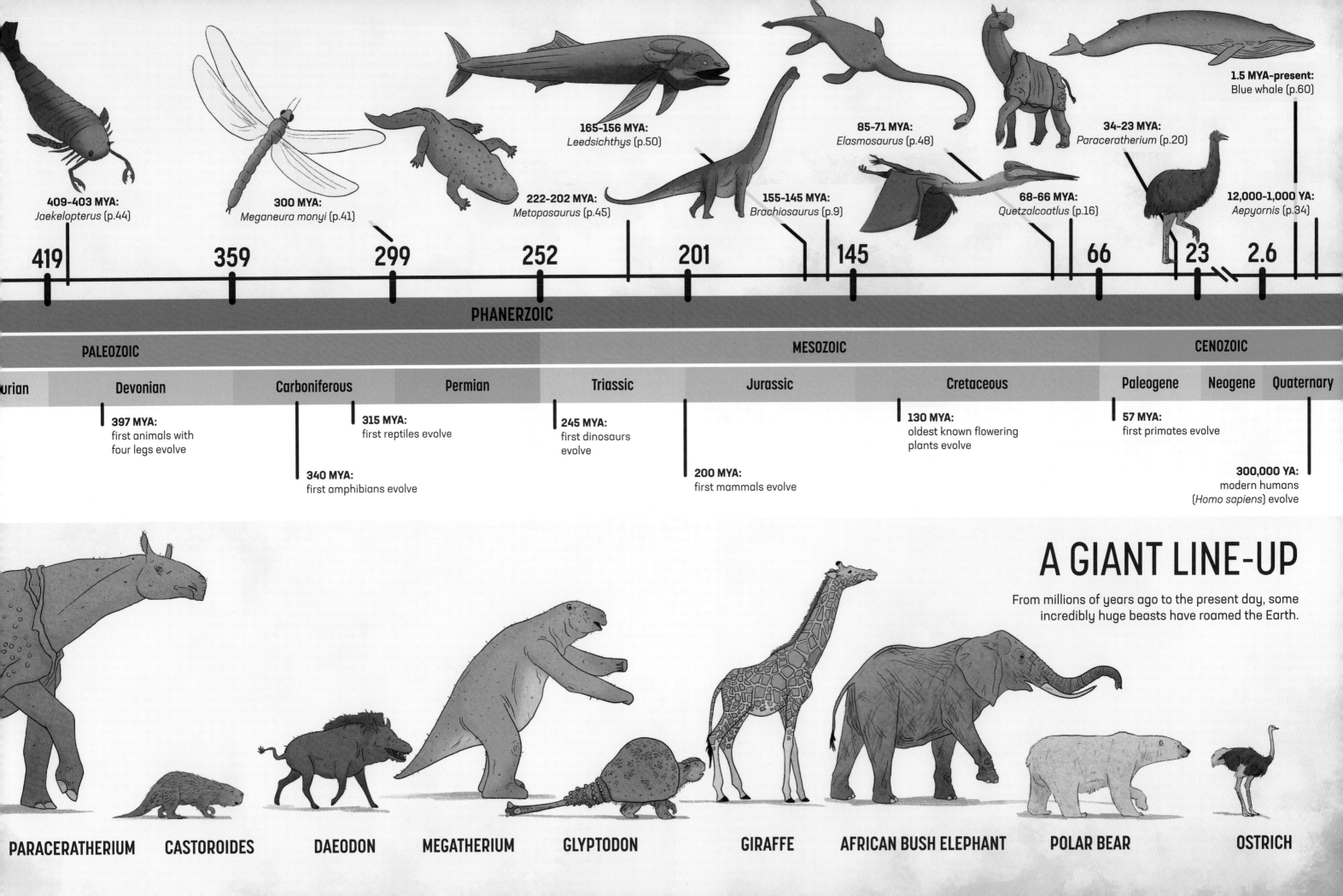

409-403 MYA:
Jaekelopterus (p.44)

300 MYA:
Meganeura monyi (p.41)

165-156 MYA:
Leedsichthys (p.50)

222-202 MYA:
Metoposaurus (p.45)

155-145 MYA:
Brachiosaurus (p.9)

85-71 MYA:
Elasmosaurus (p.48)

34-23 MYA:
Paraceratherium (p.20)

1.5 MYA-present:
Blue whale (p.60)

68-66 MYA:
Quetzalcoatlus (p.16)

12,000-1,000 YA:
Aepyornis (p.34)

419   359   299   252   201   145   66   23   2.6

PHANERZOIC

PALEOZOIC			MESOZOIC			CENOZOIC		
urian	Devonian	Carboniferous	Permian	Triassic	Jurassic	Cretaceous	Paleogene	Neogene	Quaternary

397 MYA:
first animals with
four legs evolve

315 MYA:
first reptiles evolve

245 MYA:
first dinosaurs
evolve

130 MYA:
oldest known flowering
plants evolve

57 MYA:
first primates evolve

340 MYA:
first amphibians evolve

200 MYA:
first mammals evolve

300,000 YA:
modern humans
(*Homo sapiens*) evolve

A GIANT LINE-UP

From millions of years ago to the present day, some
incredibly huge beasts have roamed the Earth.

PARACERATHERIUM   **CASTOROIDES**   **DAEODON**   **MEGATHERIUM**   **GLYPTODON**   **GIRAFFE**   **AFRICAN BUSH ELEPHANT**   **POLAR BEAR**   **OSTRICH**

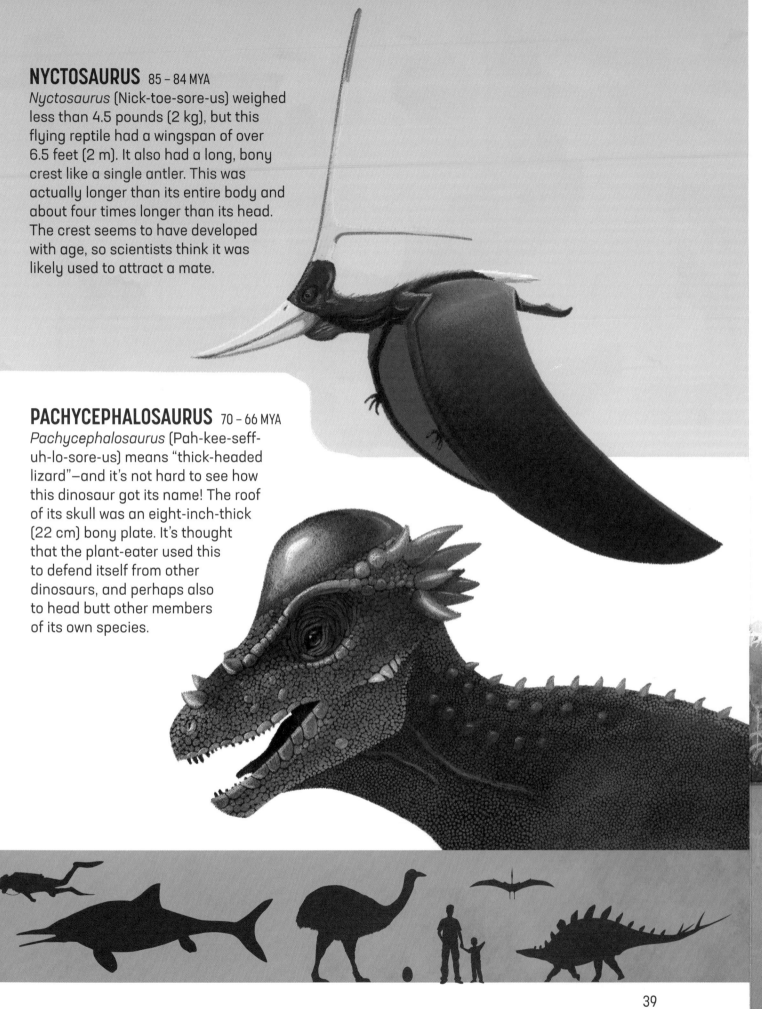

NYCTOSAURUS 85 – 84 MYA

Nyctosaurus (Nick-toe-sore-us) weighed less than 4.5 pounds (2 kg), but this flying reptile had a wingspan of over 6.5 feet (2 m). It also had a long, bony crest like a single antler. This was actually longer than its entire body and about four times longer than its head. The crest seems to have developed with age, so scientists think it was likely used to attract a mate.

PACHYCEPHALOSAURUS 70 – 66 MYA

Pachycephalosaurus (Pah-kee-seff-uh-lo-sore-us) means "thick-headed lizard"—and it's not hard to see how this dinosaur got its name! The roof of its skull was an eight-inch-thick (22 cm) bony plate. It's thought that the plant-eater used this to defend itself from other dinosaurs, and perhaps also to head butt other members of its own species.

GIANTS OF THE RIVERS & SEAS

Rivers abounded in the prehistoric world. They attracted many outsized creatures who lived in or close to their waters. Buzzing above such places around 300 million years ago was a huge relative of dragonflies—*Meganeura monyi* (mega-noor-ah mon-ee). It measured about 27 inches (68 cm) from wingtip to wingtip—about three times the span of a man's hand.

Spinosaurus 100 – 94 MYA

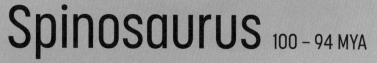

Prehistoric creatures living in and alongside rivers kept a wary eye out for this fearsome giant hunter in northern Africa around 95 million years ago.

Spinosaurus (spine-oh-sore-us) gets its name from the row of tall spines on its back. Some were over six feet (1.8 m) tall and had flaps of skin in between them to make a large sail. Scientists are not sure what the spines were for, but they likely had a role in display, making the dinosaur look much bigger and more powerful.

Spinosaurus was one of the few meat-eating dinosaurs that was bigger than *Tyrannosaurus rex*. It grew up to 50 feet (15 m) long and weighed more than 6.5 tons—the weight of nine cows. It supported its weight on two sturdy rear legs. Its front legs were smaller with short, sharp claws on its three toes.

Spinosaurus may be the first known dinosaur that could swim in water. Its bones were denser than other theropod dinosaurs' and it had a thick, long tail that may have acted like a paddle.

Its mouth was longer and thinner than *T. rex*, though, and it looked more like a giant crocodile. It mostly used its cone-shaped teeth to snap up big fish to eat. Some of the fish it caught were twice as long as you are tall!

It wasn't just fish that were attacked. *Spinosaurus*' large size means it likely ate a range of prey. Scientists think it sometimes hunted young land dinosaurs and relatives of modern day crocodiles. *Spinosaurus* may even have reared up, snapped its head around sharply, and plucked low-flying pterosaurs out of the sky with its long jaws.

Freshwater Giants

Rivers, streams, and ponds contained some wild, giant creatures in the past.

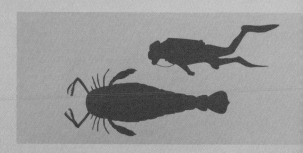

JAEKELOPTERUS 409 – 403 MYA

Long before dinosaurs roamed the Earth, a stupendous scorpion-like animal ruled the river mouths and esturies of ancient Germany. *Jaekelopterus rhenaniae* (Jay-ker-lop-tear-us ray-nay-nen-ee) was over eight feet (2.5 m) long. *Jaekelopterus* was armed with two colossal claws, 18 inches (46 cm) long, which it used to grab its food. It may have crushed its prey between its claws and strong spines on its legs that acted like teeth.

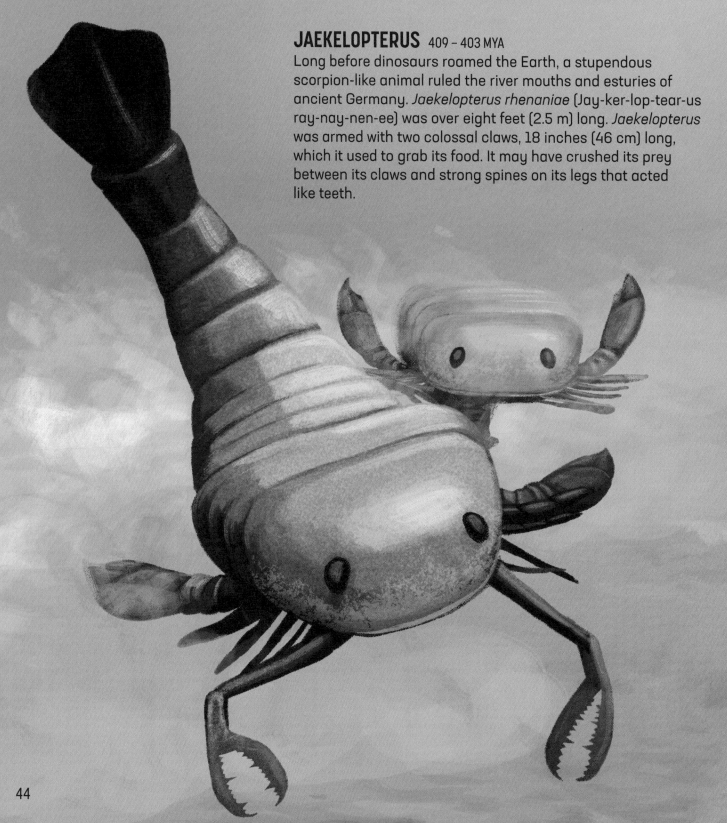

STUPENDEMYS 13 – 7 MYA

Stupendemys (Stu-pen-dem-iss) lived in the rivers and wetlands of northern South America. For a turtle, it was a whopper—at least the size of a hatchback car. Its tough, bony shell may have measured over 10 feet (3 m) long. Small horns or spikes on either side of the shell's neck opening offered further protection against other giants intent on eating turtles for dinner. *Stupendemys* ate a varied diet itself, from fruit and seeds to fish, snakes, and even alligator-like creatures called caiman.

METOPOSAURUS 222 – 202 MYA

Amphibians are creatures with backbones that need to lay their eggs in water. Most amphibians like garden frogs and newts can fit in the palm of your hand but *Metoposaurus* (Me-top-o-sore-us) certainly wouldn't. It was about the length of an automobile and weighed around 1,000 pounds (450 kg)—that's more than a grizzly bear!

The only puny thing about *Metoposaurus* was its four small, weak legs. Scientists think that it evolved to spend most of its life sitting in rivers where the water helped support its weight. There, it would wait with its broad flat mouth wide open ready to gobble up unwary river fish that swam too close.

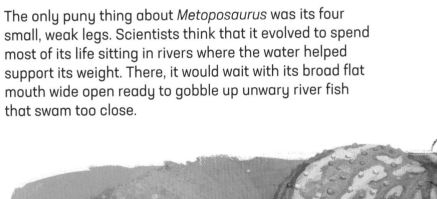

Big, Big Birds

After the dinosaurs and prehistoric flying reptiles died out 66 million years ago, other creatures took their place. Birds evolved during the age of dinosaurs but flourished after they had gone, with some reaching enormous sizes.

COLOSSUS PENGUIN 37 – 34 MYA

Approximately 12 to 14 species of penguins lived around the Antarctic 30 to 40 million years ago, but none were bigger than *Palaeeudyptes klekowskii* (Pa-lee-yoo-dip-tees clek-ow-skee)—nicknamed the colossus penguin. From head to toe, this giant bird measured about five feet (1.6 m) tall—about the same height as a person. Whereas a king penguin weighs about 33 pounds (15 kg) today, the colossus penguin tipped the scales at as much as 250 pounds (115 kg). That's about the same weight as a giant panda!

Just like modern penguins, the bird waddled around slowly on land but would have moved quickly and gracefully once in the water. Scientists believe that its great bulk and large lungs allowed it to dive underwater for up to 40 minutes with a single breath.

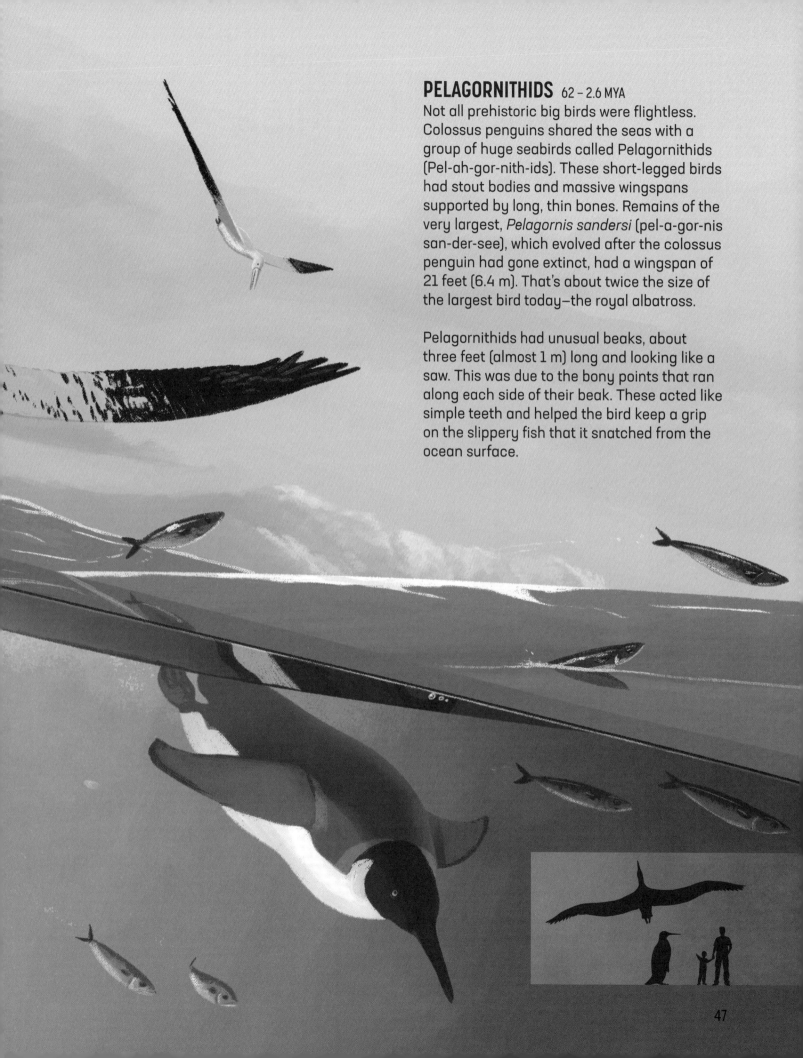

PELAGORNITHIDS 62 – 2.6 MYA

Not all prehistoric big birds were flightless. Colossus penguins shared the seas with a group of huge seabirds called Pelagornithids (Pel-ah-gor-nith-ids). These short-legged birds had stout bodies and massive wingspans supported by long, thin bones. Remains of the very largest, *Pelagornis sandersi* (pel-a-gor-nis san-der-see), which evolved after the colossus penguin had gone extinct, had a wingspan of 21 feet (6.4 m). That's about twice the size of the largest bird today—the royal albatross.

Pelagornithids had unusual beaks, about three feet (almost 1 m) long and looking like a saw. This was due to the bony points that ran along each side of their beak. These acted like simple teeth and helped the bird keep a grip on the slippery fish that it snatched from the ocean surface.

Monster Marine Reptiles

Dangers lurked below the sea surface for any unwary prehistoric fish or other sea creature. Some gigantic underwater hunters had huge appetites that needed feeding, including these two monstrous marine reptiles from 80 or so million years ago.

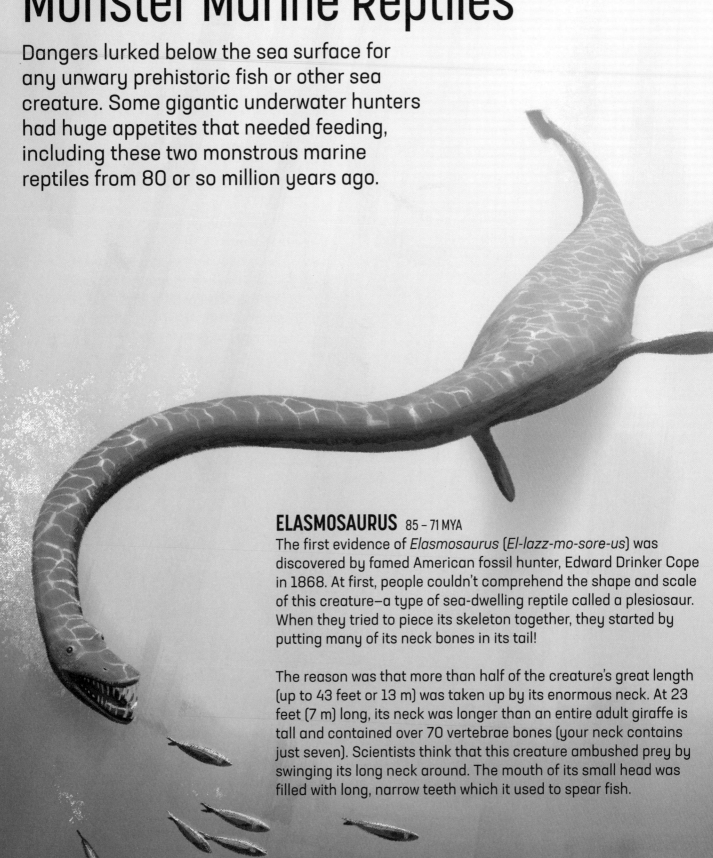

ELASMOSAURUS 85 – 71 MYA

The first evidence of *Elasmosaurus* (*El-lazz-mo-sore-us*) was discovered by famed American fossil hunter, Edward Drinker Cope in 1868. At first, people couldn't comprehend the shape and scale of this creature—a type of sea-dwelling reptile called a plesiosaur. When they tried to piece its skeleton together, they started by putting many of its neck bones in its tail!

The reason was that more than half of the creature's great length (up to 43 feet or 13 m) was taken up by its enormous neck. At 23 feet (7 m) long, its neck was longer than an entire adult giraffe is tall and contained over 70 vertebrae bones (your neck contains just seven). Scientists think that this creature ambushed prey by swinging its long neck around. The mouth of its small head was filled with long, narrow teeth which it used to spear fish.

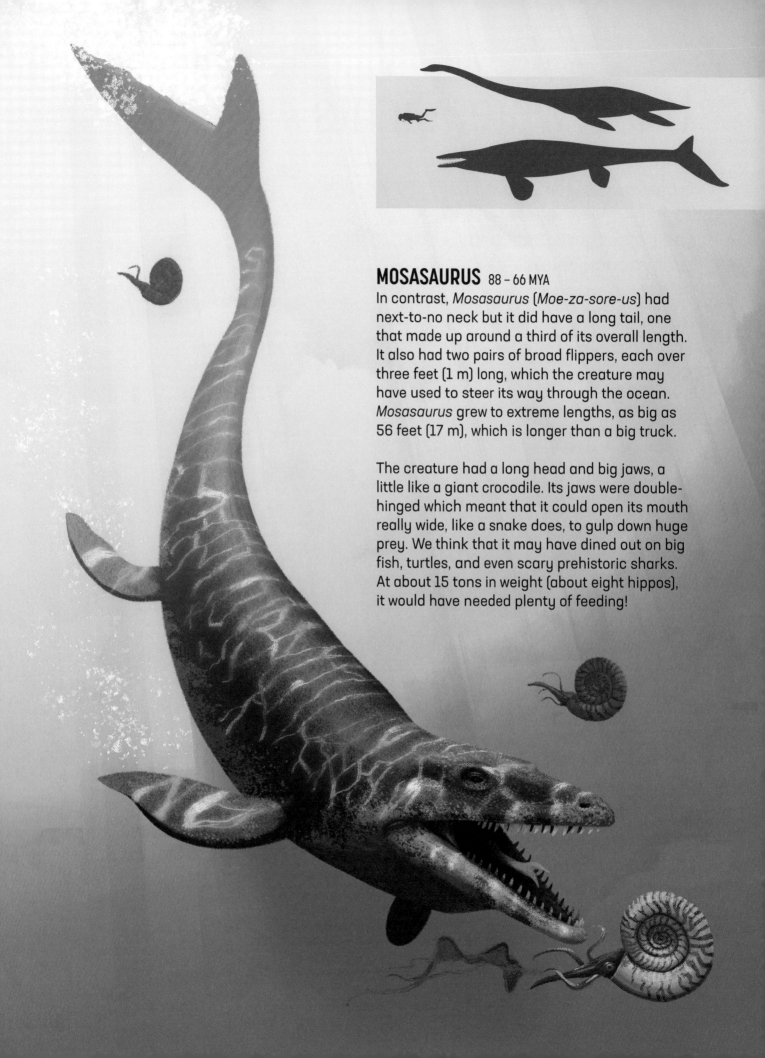

MOSASAURUS 88 – 66 MYA

In contrast, *Mosasaurus* (*Moe-za-sore-us*) had next-to-no neck but it did have a long tail, one that made up around a third of its overall length. It also had two pairs of broad flippers, each over three feet (1 m) long, which the creature may have used to steer its way through the ocean. *Mosasaurus* grew to extreme lengths, as big as 56 feet (17 m), which is longer than a big truck.

The creature had a long head and big jaws, a little like a giant crocodile. Its jaws were double-hinged which meant that it could open its mouth really wide, like a snake does, to gulp down huge prey. We think that it may have dined out on big fish, turtles, and even scary prehistoric sharks. At about 15 tons in weight (about eight hippos), it would have needed plenty of feeding!

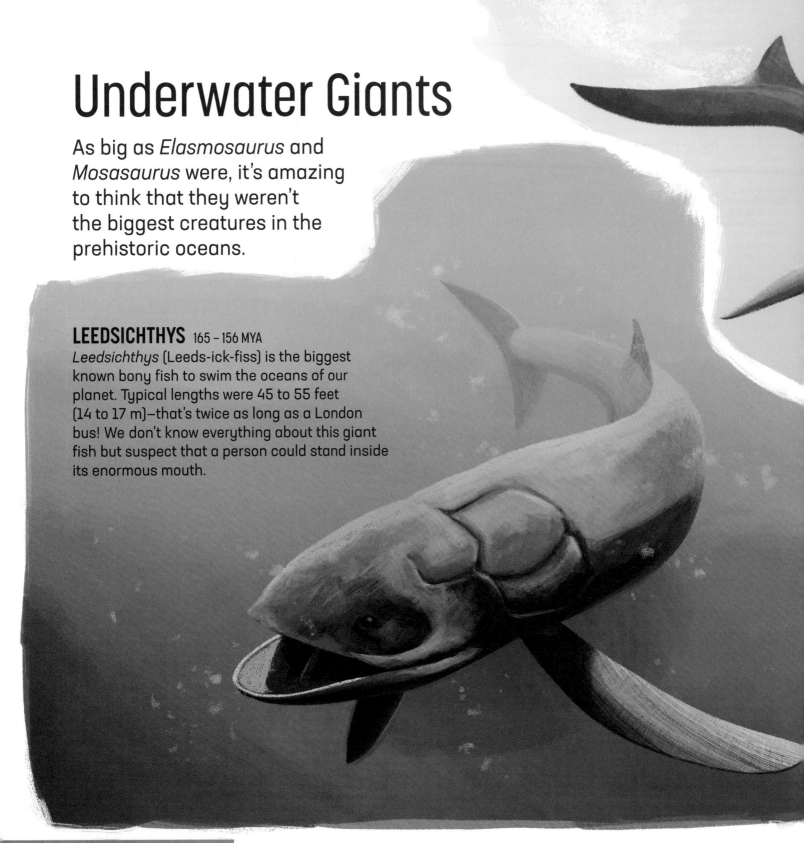

Underwater Giants

As big as *Elasmosaurus* and *Mosasaurus* were, it's amazing to think that they weren't the biggest creatures in the prehistoric oceans.

LEEDSICHTHYS 165 – 156 MYA

Leedsichthys (Leeds-ick-fiss) is the biggest known bony fish to swim the oceans of our planet. Typical lengths were 45 to 55 feet (14 to 17 m)—that's twice as long as a London bus! We don't know everything about this giant fish but suspect that a person could stand inside its enormous mouth.

Leedsichthys was a filter feeder. It used mesh plates called rakers to sieve out zooplankton and other tiny creatures from the huge gulps of sea water its giant mouth took. This way of feeding is the method used today by some whales and basking sharks.

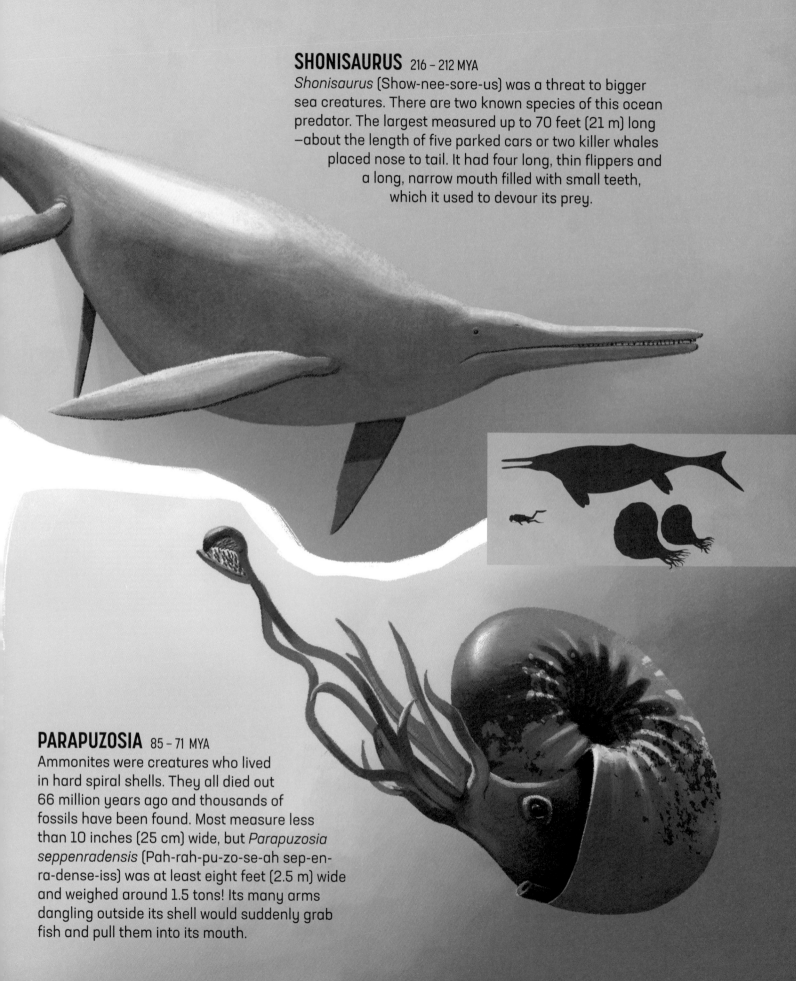

SHONISAURUS 216 – 212 MYA

Shonisaurus (Show-nee-sore-us) was a threat to bigger sea creatures. There are two known species of this ocean predator. The largest measured up to 70 feet (21 m) long —about the length of five parked cars or two killer whales placed nose to tail. It had four long, thin flippers and a long, narrow mouth filled with small teeth, which it used to devour its prey.

PARAPUZOSIA 85 – 71 MYA

Ammonites were creatures who lived in hard spiral shells. They all died out 66 million years ago and thousands of fossils have been found. Most measure less than 10 inches (25 cm) wide, but *Parapuzosia seppenradensis* (Pah-rah-pu-zo-se-ah sep-en-ra-dense-iss) was at least eight feet (2.5 m) wide and weighed around 1.5 tons! Its many arms dangling outside its shell would suddenly grab fish and pull them into its mouth.

GIANTS OF TODAY

Many enormous creatures—from the hundreds of different dinosaurs that once existed to mammoths and flying pterosaurs—have all died out. Some amazing animal giants, though, are still with us. A lot are endangered and need people's help to protect them and their homes if we are to enjoy these astounding creatures in the future.

Some modern giants, such as the fearsome saltwater crocodile, are thankfully not under threat. The biggest saltwater crocodiles can grow up to 20 feet (6.5 m) long. They often lurk in shallow waters at the edge of rivers and estuaries, ready to pounce.

African Elephant

The African bush elephant is the largest land animal in the world. Males can stand 13 feet (4 m) tall and weigh 6.5 tons. Even babies are heavy. A newborn elephant calf can weigh 265 pounds (120 kg). That's the same as 300 cans of baked beans! It takes them a long time to reach their full size—around 35 to 40 years. To get so big requires a lot of eating—by the time an elephant reaches adulthood, it will eat at least 220 pounds (100 kg) of food each day.

An elephant's trunk is packed full of muscle. This makes it heavy but capable of lifting 530 pounds (240 kg)—that's the weight of three wolves. Their trunk can handle delicate objects as well as sucking up two gallons (8 l) of water at once to then squirt it into their mouth. Some elephants even use their trunk as a snorkel to breathe when crossing rivers.

An elephant's skin is one inch (2.5 cm) thick, but can suffer from sunburn. To avoid this, elephants take regular mud baths, showering themselves with mud, sand, and dust to protect their skin. Their huge tusks can reach 6.5 feet (2 m) long and are actually overgrown teeth. They make useful tools to dig up plant roots or strip bark off trees but, unfortunately, they are also highly prized by poachers, who have killed thousands of these magnificent creatures.

Big Bears

Among the eight species of bears alive today are several majestic big beasts.

POLAR BEAR

Mighty polar bears stalk the Arctic on the lookout for fish and seals to eat. Their keen sense of smell can sniff out a seal from more than half a mile away. The largest four-legged land predator currently on Earth, a male polar bear can weigh over 1,300 pounds (600 kg). When it rears up, it can measure as much as 11.5 feet (3.5 m) tall—twice the average height of a man.

Polar bears like to roam and can travel more than 600 miles (1,000 km) in a month. That's like walking from London to Spain. The soles of their big, 12-inch-wide (30 cm) paws are covered in small bumps and dips which act like suction cups to help them grip the ice. They're also good swimmers and can paddle for days at a time using their front legs. They're protected from the cold by a thick layer of body fat and two layers of fur. Sometimes, when winds are especially fierce, they dig a hole in a bank of snow and snuggle up in it, curling themselves up into a tight ball.

KODIAK BEAR

No brown bears quite get to the size of the biggest polar bear, except for the Kodiak bear. This is so named because it lives on the Kodiak chain of islands off the coast of Alaska, cut off from the continents for 12,000 years. The bears here grew large, although they start off pretty small. When born, they weigh less than a small bag of sugar (one pound or 450 g) but within three months reach 20 times that weight.

By the time they are fully grown, eating salmon, berries, and other foods, male Kodiak bears can weigh over 1,000 pounds (500 kg) and, now and then, over 1,300 pounds (600 kg). When standing on their hind legs, they can rear up to ten feet (3 m) tall—making an impressive and scary sight.

Plains Giants

The grassy plains, rivers, and waterholes of Africa are home today to many of the world's biggest surviving land mammals and birds.

HIPPOPOTAMUS

The hippopotamus can grow up to 16.5 feet (5 m) long and weigh up to two tons. Despite spending most of their day in the water, hippos can't actually swim. They can submerge themselves, though, and hold their breath for five minutes. At night, they leave the water to graze on grass and plants, often eating 90 pounds (40 kg) of food each night. A hippo can open its jaws really wide—about 150 degrees (humans can barely manage 50 degrees)—creating a space big enough for a child to crawl in!

GIRAFFE

The giraffe is the tallest animal on Earth, standing 18 feet (5.5 m) high. That's about as tall as four people standing on each other's shoulders. Giraffes are surprisingly nimble and can run at 25 mles (40 km) per hour for several kilometres at a time. What they're not so good at is bending down to take a drink at a stream or waterhole. Luckily, giraffes get most of the moisture they need from the plants they eat, which they often grip and pull into their mouths using their strong, purple, 20-inch-long (50 cm) tongues.

OSTRICH

Ostriches can reach nine feet (2.75 m) tall and the biggest weigh as much as two men. These flightless birds have muscular legs and feet, each with only two toes, that help make them really fast runners. An adult ostrich can sprint at over 40 miles (65 km) per hour for short stretches, but can also run at around 25 miles (40 km) per hour for many miles at a time. When running fast they can use their wings like a rudder to help them steer and change direction.

Giants of the Deep

The oceans contain some of the most incredible life, including the largest known creature to ever live on Earth—the blue whale.

BLUE WHALE

About the size of a small jet airliner, blue whales grow up to 100 feet (30 m) long. Some blue whales tip the scales at 200 tons. That's the same weight as 40 monster trucks, 25 *Triceratops* dinosaurs, or around 2,600 men. The whale's tail is as wide as a full-sized soccer goal.

One of the few parts of a blue whale that seem undersized is its eyes—they're only the size of a grapefruit. Baby blue whales are born big, weighing over two tons and measuring 23 feet (7 m) long. A baby can guzzle up to 95 gallons (360 l) of milk (almost three bathtub's worth) from its mother every day. All this food helps it to grow fast. As an adult, it has to eat up to 4.5 tons of tiny shrimp-like creatures called krill each day to keep its weight up!

COLOSSAL SQUID

This deep-sea dweller has been found up to 6,600 feet (2,000 m) below the ocean surface. It can weigh over half a ton, grow 33 feet (10 m) long, and possesses gigantic eyeballs, bigger than a basketball, for peering through the gloom. Its long tentacles are covered with suckers and hooks to snare prey such as fish and other squids.

MANTA RAY

This giant fish is shaped like a diamond, measures 23 feet (7 m) wide, and weighs two tons—as much as a white rhino. Playful and smart, they feast on plankton and other small sea creatures and can dive to depths of hundreds of feet.

JAPANESE SPIDER CRAB

Looking like something from a science fiction movie, the world's largest crab has a 12.5-foot (3.8 m) leg span and can weigh up to 45 pounds (20 kg). It covers its body with algae and sea sponges to camouflage itself in deep water.

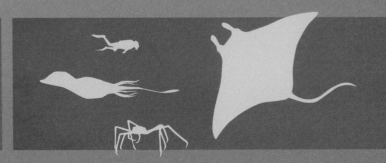

The Biggest of their Kind

Few creatures today are anywhere near as big as a colossal squid or a manta ray but they can be the biggest of their type. These notable creatures include insects, amphibians, bats, and lizards. Take a look at some of these incredible giants —perhaps one day you might see a giant in the wild for yourself!

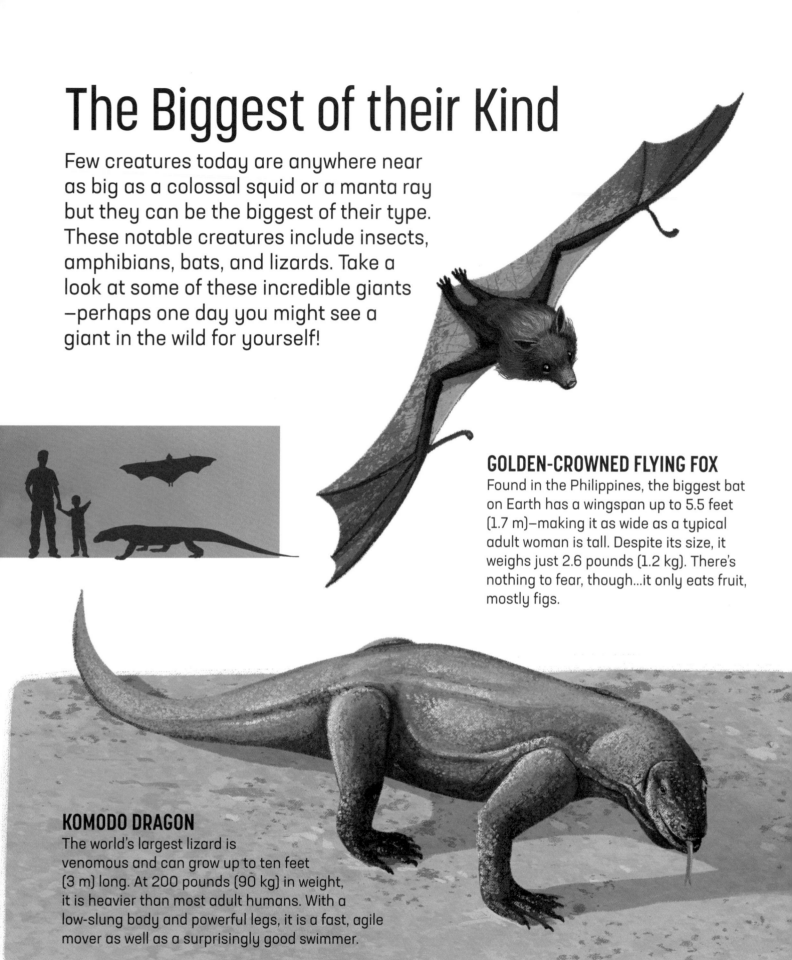

GOLDEN-CROWNED FLYING FOX
Found in the Philippines, the biggest bat on Earth has a wingspan up to 5.5 feet (1.7 m)—making it as wide as a typical adult woman is tall. Despite its size, it weighs just 2.6 pounds (1.2 kg). There's nothing to fear, though...it only eats fruit, mostly figs.

KOMODO DRAGON
The world's largest lizard is venomous and can grow up to ten feet (3 m) long. At 200 pounds (90 kg) in weight, it is heavier than most adult humans. With a low-slung body and powerful legs, it is a fast, agile mover as well as a surprisingly good swimmer.

GOLIATH FROG

A frog that weighs as much as a cat sounds crazy, but this 12.5-inch-long (32 cm), 7.3 pound (3.3 kg) amphibian is an absolute whopper. Despite its bulk, it can make large leaps, ten feet (3 m) in length, and catch insects speedily using its fast-moving sticky tongue. An adult will eat pretty much anything that fits in its mouth, from insects and fish, to crabs, other frogs, and even small snakes!

GOLIATH BIRDEATER

The bulkiest, heaviest spider on the planet, this tarantula spider lives in South American swamps and eats mice, frogs, and insects as well as birds. Its body can reach seven inches (18 cm) long while its eight legs give it a span of 11 inches (28 cm)—bigger than a basketball.

CHAN'S MEGASTICK

Found by an amateur insect collector in the rainforests of Borneo, Indonesia, this stick insect is really, really long—up to 21.5 inches (55 cm), with long, thin legs. The creature's quarter-inch-long (5 mm) eggs each have a pair of little wings which catch the wind. This allows the baby stick insect to grow up some distance away from its parents, so it doesn't compete with them for food.

QUEEN ALEXANDRA'S BIRDWING

This beautiful butterfly grows from an egg just a sixth of an inch (4 mm) long, into a 12-inch-wide (30 cm) adult—the largest known butterfly.

Index